GLOSS

Saint Julian Press

Poetry

PRAISE for GLOSS

Her touch is as delicate as the family silver, and as tough as the family secrets. Her meanings are as richly ambiguous as the word "gloss" itself, polishing, concealing, interpreting. All those shinings at the surface of things, and all those thready, stony rivulets in a family history, a history of mothers and grandmothers and great-grandmothers and aunts, involving years of posh and poverty—Barker sets them out as on a showcase framed in silk, with the double gloss of precision and compassion.

~ Alicia Ostriker
Author of *Waiting for the Light*

In *Gloss*, Wendy Barker meditates on the vagaries of memory, the tidal pull of family lore, the complexities of national identity, and the marvelous, often painful, interactions of three generations of women over many decades. With formal inventiveness, a story teller's eye for detail, and a profound understanding of the way deep family history lives inside us all, Barker has written a truly memorable collection of poems, one I will return to again with great pleasure.

~ Kevin Prufer
Author of *How He Loved Them*

Investigating the currents of her inheritance from England, Barker shows how intricately language and narrative mark identity. Britishisms and Americanisms become entwined in the struggle of women in her family to live according to their own choices. The images speak to one another from inside the lines of elegance versus roughness, and questions of what is genuine. Where there is critical unearthing there is also compassion. The feeling of the book is neither contrite nor without apology. It is the certain fact of being this woman, a poet who summons the figure of Cordelia in understanding how we come to be, despite the fact of not being seen by the objects of our adoration, whose eyes do not know the true heart. In the definite elegance that appears in this poetic appeal to questions of who we are, Barker troubles *"These stories no one speaks. How we're silenced, mute." Gloss* is a splendidly honest work, where the lines breathe courage in the air beyond time.

~ Afaa M. Weaver
Author of *Spirit Boxing*

In crystalline images Wendy Barker unwraps the tightly wrapped package of her mother's story, each layer exposing more and more, as she turns from her mother to her grandmother's disastrous and romantic life, all the while showing how mothers pass on their beauty and fears to their daughters. In this deep and resonant book stories are gotten wrong, nightmares erupt, and secrets can finally be spoken. Barker weaves prose poems and verse into an elegant tapestry of the pentimento of one woman's life.

~ Barbara Hamby
Author of *Bird Odyssey*

Wendy Barker's *Gloss* utilizes the lyric form to conduct an archaeological dig, a profound excavation. With wit and candor, the poet unspools the narratives of three generations of women to create a family portrait that is vivid, complex, and sometimes shocking. *Gloss* sifts through the mud of personal history in a quest for the "patterns" that might provide us with answers to the universal question, "how do we become what we are?"

~ Vincent Toro
Author of *Stereo. Island. Mosaic.*

GLOSS

Poems

by

WENDY BARKER

SAINT JULIAN PRESS
HOUSTON

Published by
SAINT JULIAN PRESS, Inc.
2053 Cortlandt, Suite 200
Houston, Texas 77008

www.saintjulianpress.com

COPYRIGHT © 2020
TWO THOUSAND AND TWENTY
© Wendy Barker

ISBN-13: 978-1-7320542-5-7
ISBN: 1-7320542-5-8
Library of Congress Control Number: 2019941092

Cover Photograph: *Watermark 18* by Peter Shefler
from his *Watermarks* album.
Author Photograph by Sue Hum

In loving memory of my mother

Pamela Dodwell Bean

July 28, 1917- April 9, 2004

"Where does the present start, if it isn't in the past?"
—John Koethe, *Ninety-Fifth Street*

"You can't put the past behind you. It's buried in you; it's turned your flesh into its own cupboard."
—Claudia Rankine, *Citizen*

"I don't very much care what people do as long as they don't do it in the street and frighten the horses."
—King Edward VII

CONTENTS

∞

On the Chinese Scroll	1
What Surfaces	2
Along a River	3

∞

The RMS Queen Mary	7
The Silver Tureen (1)	8
Treading the Boards	9
Little Pieces of String Too Small To Be Used	10

∞

This Far Downstream	15
Sunday Lunch at Mom's Cousin Dinnie's: June 1969	16
Is His Boat Strong	18

∞

Silk Roads	21
The Silver Tureen (2)	23
Below the Salt	24
Ivory Carvings	25
Accounting for Granny	27

∞

Perhaps the Man   31
"Elegant," She Said   32
Maybe His Boat   34

∞

Mining Silver   37
Stiff Upper Lip   38
Interior   41
Silver Handles, Spouts   42
Latent Image   43

∞

But Even These   47
Surgery, a Little History   48
How a Surface   51

∞

The Silver Tureen (3)   55
Now I Learn   56
Gathering Bones   57
Foldings   59
Her Lists   61
Incest   63
Bird Songs   64

∞

Perhaps Upstream	67
Beyond a Certain Age, I Look for Paris in Paris	68
The Scroll's Landscape	71

GLOSS

ON THE CHINESE SCROLL

*a man in a boat
moves upstream toward
mountains—mist, with his
thin back bent, as he
faces the water
that flows from the hills
to the downstream pool
where he casts his thread-
slender line, alone.*

WHAT SURFACES

Another chip in the white enameled sink, only three years old. How
                I've tried to keep it pristine, and yet—
    stainless steel pots scrape it till the black
cast iron breaks through. What's below a surface gloss. Now the flesh
                on my hands has grown so thin
    the layers underneath show through,
rivery veins and knobby metacarpals. Knuckles like pebbles—like
                rocks. I've bordered my rose beds
    with stones from Blanco Creek. How long
did it take to shape those irregular rounds and ovals? Our house, built
                of blocks mined from the quarry only
    five miles up the road—limestone
formed in the Paleozoic Era. My favorite paperweight: a fossilized
                clam I found in the backyard, remains
    from the time the land around us
lived under ocean. Something so pocked, wizened, holding my papers
                in place. Arriving at the Grand Canyon,
    we've all peered down at those
dozens of rock layers—granite, dolomite, sandstone, shale, basalt—
                formed two million, maybe two billion
    years ago. And who would want
to mend that great magenta-, purple-, blood-shaded rip in the earth's
                surface? It's what we come for,
    to gawk at all those layers, exposed.

ALONG A RIVER

*you will know upstream
from downstream. Off these
sloped banks, clumped water
hyacinths, mossy
strands provide clues, no
movement other than
scarlet dragonflies
flitting the surface,
mosquitoes. Beyond,
a source you must find.*

THE RMS QUEEN MARY

Docked since '67 in Long Beach, the same liner Mom sailed in '39 from England to marry my father. Relic of a past the well-heeled now are recreating, "cruise" being the upscale way for travel, like the tour labeled "Alaska's Glorious Inside Passage in 8 Days," or the one advertised as "Wonders of the Mekong, 10 Days Down South Asia's Amazing River." But the Queen Mary was not designed for this sort of travel, rather to get you from Southampton to New York in less than a week.

Or from one life to another. Within a year Mom had lost most of her Britishisms, but not all. "Oh, you Americans," she'd shudder at us daughters, though she carried on with Thanksgiving and the Fourth of July. The phrase "carry on" holds more weight than hand luggage. Alone on the Queen Mary. Not part of any migration. No soft-bosomed granny, no jocular uncles to keep her afloat. Those glossy first-class cabins were kept spotless. Then repainted, reupholstered, refurbished. Not a trace of her.

THE SILVER TUREEN (1)

It keeps slamming open, exposing the tangled roots of garlic I store inside it. How often my father quoted Lear's praise of Cordelia: "Her voice was ever soft and low, an excellent thing in woman." Better dead than loud. The tureen won't stay shut. Garlic smell throughout the house. And, of course, it's prettier when closed. Glossier, sleeker. The polished dome like a perfect loaf of risen bread, or a silky breast. Sleek, smooth, easy to run a hand over, no sharp edges.

TREADING THE BOARDS

What Great Granny Lilian Graves did before she became respectable. Or what she did after she'd been respectable, after her husband died of drink, leaving her penniless with four little ones. She farmed them out to relatives and went on stage. Ravishing, like Mom's mother and Mom herself, Great Granny danced, sang, and acted wherever she could. Even in America, in Tombstone, where she held the stage of the Bird Cage Theater with Buffalo Bill Cody, "a *charming* man," she once told Mom with a little smile. Where was it she caught Prince Edward's eye? London? Paris? After he tired of her, he set her up with Mr. Graves, who needed a research assistant. And why not a wife as well? The Bird Cage Theater to the British Museum. Later, widowed, she'd let my mother visit, served her tea. Mom would sneak up to London on the train, disobeying her mummy who'd tried to keep a daughter from this disgraceful woman who'd abandoned her children for a life of shame. "When you go out to Hong Kong, my dear," Great Granny told my seventeen-year-old mother, "you must buy black lace underwear. They do such things exquisitely."

"LITTLE PIECES OF STRING TOO SMALL TO BE USED"

Granny's label on a box in her attic. Four dozen cardboard boxes, filed alphabetically. And all tied with string. How Mom laughed about Granny, but when at bedtime I'd beg her to tell about her growing up in England, she'd brush my forehead with a quick, dry kiss, tuck the sheet around my shoulders, close my door.

Under the covers, with a flashlight, I read and reread the books Granny sent, about two West Berkshire kids in the '30s. Was Mom's childhood like theirs? The novels came in a parcel tied with knots so tight we had to use scissors, so by the time we'd unwrapped the box, bits of string littered the cement floor. I'd thank Granny on white blue-lined paper with my Parker fountain pen, and she'd answer on tissue-thin blue paper, stamps of Queen Elizabeth on the envelopes. I even wrote to Grace James, the books' author, and she wrote back on paper just like Granny's, telling me what happened to those children when they grew up, and explaining the stories behind the stories. I kept those pieces of thin blue paper, a tidy stack in my bedside drawer. But not wrapped with string.

Now in an old box, I've found a letter dated 1934, addressed to Mrs. Jacoby, Headmistress at Battle Abbey, Mom's "public" school. My mother's exam scores had been outstanding and could Mom's parents let her enter Cambridge, where, the letter writer was confident, Mom would "go far." But, as Mom told me once, no college for girls of her "class," no "bluestockings" in their family, and she needed to be presented at court instead, a distinction naughty Mom rejected.

My first trip home from college my bedside drawer was empty, all those blue letters gone. Have to get rid of old things, Mom said, her toes flapping the soles of her sandals.

That was after my father hadn't let me accept the scholarships I'd been offered from "good" colleges Back East. As a girl, I'd be a "bad investment" since I'd only be getting married anyway. I never kept the letters with those offers, not in a box or a drawer. Daddy did agree to pay for tuition and board at the nearby state school he'd always sneered at.

I don't remember when I carried all my diaries, notebooks, and stories out to the galvanized can in the garage. Ripped the pages into bits, everything I'd ever written. Little pieces. Too small to be used. Tossed them in. No amount of string could have held them together. Or me, at the end of my rope.

∞

THIS FAR DOWNSTREAM

*small leaves appear
distinct—pinnate,
alternate, whorled—
you can see how
they are joined to
the primary
vein, the leaf's mid-
rib, the patterns,
the direction
as they're facing
beyond the stem.*

SUNDAY LUNCH AT MOM'S COUSIN DINNIE'S: JUNE 1969

I'd barely recovered from a concussive first year teaching ninth-grade
English in West Berkeley, from ear-shattering
shrieks, "Mothuh Fuckin Honky Bitch" rattling steel
lockers, but here we were, on my first trip to my mother's homeland,
pulled up in a rented Morris Mini at a gray stone,
rose-trellised, three-story house in Windsor. And here
they were, Dinnie and husband Jack in tweeds with their three grown
kids lined up by the arched entrance. I'd heard
about Dinnie for years, how, during the late thirties,
Mom lived with Dinnie's family in Hong Kong where the cousins
crooned a breathy Andrews Sisters knock-off
act for the fellows in the Royal Navy. Now this
silver-haired, brogue-shod, square-shouldered woman was striding up
to my mother, murmuring "Pamela darling," in
a voice so exquisitely muted you couldn't have known
they hadn't seen each other in thirty years. The two exchanged pristine
pecks on the cheek. Lunch was a limp white fish
with hand-picked peas from the garden and boiled
potatoes on gold-rimmed china. Conversation perked along politely,
like water just shy of a full boil. Asked about
my students, I tried to explain: a half mile from
the Black Panthers' headquarters, Telegraph Avenue, pimps, Black
Muslims, acid-dropping by the train tracks,
but then Penelope, Dinnie's eldest, just back
from her posh au-pair gig in Provence, asked: "What *ever* do you do
about their accents? They must be dreadful!"
she moaned. I know I came close to spitting

a mouthful of potatoes onto the linen table cloth. Now I think of
             the way Mom, after sixty years in the States,
    still fussed about British accents that didn't
approach RP standards. And I couldn't have told that young woman
             almost my age that I'd spent years trying to
    flatten the lilting upper-crust British intonations
I'd learned at my mother's knee, and that I'd begun saying "How ya
             doin," and "Gimme five," even grinning at
    "Sheee-it, Man" coming from the coaches
at lunch. And I couldn't have explained that, as we hustled students
             out of the building while hall guards searched
    for the bomb reported in somebody's locker,
I wasn't fussing about accents. I've been away from Berkeley now as
             many years as Mom had lived in the States
    before our lunch with Dinnie, and after three
decades in Texas, I know I drag out my vowels, multiplying dipthongs
             into tripthongs. In fact, a Brooklyn friend has
    fondly mentioned my "soothing Southern accent." My
mother would have been horrified. I'd like to see Penelope again. Both
             our mothers are gone. I heard her granddaughter's
    dating a guy from Jamaica who's into trip hop.

IS HIS BOAT STRONG

*enough to reach
up such a long
river with turns
beyond the first
rock ledge where all
the trees' branches
sharpen, before
the waters deepen?*

∞

SILK ROADS

Such a quiet act, the needle penetrating cloth. Loops of thread in coral, pink, fuchsia, teal, turquoise, forest green, lime, lemon, mustard, royal purple, brown, and black. The design dotted in crisp dark blue on the linen. A butterfly, a road.

The Great Silk Road. Overland. But by the time my great grandfather set off mid-nineteenth century to find more silk for Macclesfield's mills in Cheshire, he traveled by sea. The story goes he sailed up the Yangtze to ask the Chinese to trade. But how far upriver and on what sort of boat?

All from a worm, the caterpillar of a moth. Larvae of silverfish, wasps, mayflies, lacewings, and thrips produce silk, too, though not of good quality. Not used for textiles. And not for embroidery. Glossy three-ply filaments satin-stitching, chain-stitching leaves, wings, ridges in a winding path.

The prow of a ship cutting through water, the spray of droplets glistening in the light. A steel needle pricking the gaps between the woven linen threads, the needle emerging from underneath, poked back to the surface.

I don't know what Great Grandfather offered to trade for silk, only that the Chinese told him to go back where he came from. But overnight a typhoon ripped the current. In the morning, village elders boarded the battered ship, said they'd trade with this white devil, the spirits had willed it.

The pupas are dipped in boiling water or pierced with a needle. Then the cocoon is unraveled as a continuous thread. How a boat knifes its way through a current, lifting ripples, a wake. I want to slice through this story, unspool its lengths. Great-Grandfather didn't speak Mandarin. Who translated? Who traveled with him? Did trackers drag the ship through shallows, narrows of the Yangtze's Three Gorges, hauling that weight? And who paid whom for what?

Some embroideries are never finished. And even if we try to keep the underside tidy, to avoid messy knots and threads, it's hard to see a pattern on the back of the cloth, where the colors, even while shimmering, snarl.

THE SILVER TUREEN (2)

I never know when it will come crashing open, the domed lid swiveling back into the curved underside, like a pistol shot. Just shuffling past in my slippers as it sits on those four spindly grooved legs and *wham*, there it goes. I've never used it for soup, never for serving, only for storing garlic.

Which my mother hated. As she did "pasta" (which she pronounced the way she did "disaster") and anything Italian, though she'd sure cooked up plenty of macaroni and cheese casseroles when we were kids, when I didn't know a tureen from a cereal bowl. It was my New Jersey grandma's, round-bellied altarpiece of her high-ceilinged dining room, standing between the crystal candelabras atop her mahogany buffet. But I never saw it holding soup, either vichyssoise or Campbell's cream of tomato.

A lid like a mouth. Mouthing off. You and your big mouth. My father, sniping at Mom, "You don't know what you're talking about." Opening his mouth to shut hers. Keep your trap shut. That woman's got a mouth on her. There you go again, flapping your jaw.

I'm thinking of plants' stomata—"stoma," from the Greek for "mouth"—opening and closing as light and humidity shift, a silent way, inspiration and expiration, a breathing. All through the day. Not like this sudden, metallic crash. As if something no one wanted to hear is shrieked out loud. There it goes again. And I wasn't even close.

BELOW THE SALT

Granny's place before she married. A governess, helping the parlour maid polish silver before the house parties. At one of them, she met Grandfather. Sometimes the mistress let her join the grown-ups for supper, though mostly Granny nibbled buttered toast and a coddled egg upstairs with the children. Later, wife of the Chairman of the Board, she shrank from fancy dinners. From beaded, sequined dresses, from perfume and cleavage. Sent my adolescent mother instead. Grandfather escorted her on his arm, his stunning daughter, wrapped in silver fox and satin, her chocolate brown eyes, creamy skin—almost white as the salt.

IVORY CARVINGS

How it swelled in the bathroom sink, Granny's cardboard pellet. A basin full of water, and then, a slow unfurling—petals, a lotus. And more petals, rose, lavender, yellow, abloom in the chipped sink we spat in while brushing our teeth.

The lotus petals signal an expansion of the soul. Or were those paper flowers chrysanthemums? For Confucius, objects of meditation. In China even now, symbols of vitality.

For years on my living room wall—in intricate high relief, nine inches in diameter—a chrysanthemum made of ivory, poised on its stem, and set on a black background in a two-by-five-foot frame. Once it hung in Granny's high-ceilinged hallway in Hong Kong. Carved from an elephant's tusk.

How these creatures mourn their dead, circle the body, caress it with their trunks. Flap their ears, click their tusks, entwine their trunks when reuniting. Big money for those tusks, long, curved incisors. White gold.

Favorite bedtime reading, in Granny's voice, "O Best Beloved," how the elephant's child got his trunk, a painful stretching of his little nose by a crocodile. No mention of his tusks, although in Kipling's drawing they're right there, both of them, pointing toward a banana tree.

By the tenth century, not an elephant left in North Africa. Now from Kenya to Congo to Cameroon, mass killings daily. In Tanzania, villagers roll poisoned pumpkins into the road for elephants to eat.

Bananas—shaped like small tusks. Granny's collection of bric-a-brac included a banana carved from ivory. So clever, she'd say, the way the artist showed it half peeled, as if ready to eat. The petals of my ivory chrysanthemum—a mandala? Or a mouth forced open, jagged stumps, splinters of teeth?

ACCOUNTING FOR GRANNY

All the places she lived. First in Wales, Glagmorganshire, till her alcoholic father died. Then sent to South London—raised by an aunt who'd married the Vicar of St. Peter's Parish. Then at fifteen, hired as a governess. Even lived with her "family" in Shimla—she loved India, Mom said. Then Grandfather, China, and a succession of houses.

The one Mom showed me on my first trip to England: four stories, with a drive long as the street I live on now, past rows of beech trees bordering vegetable gardens, greenhouses, rose gardens, and kennels, swooping up to the manor's stone arched entrance. The whole top story, Mom said, for the servants. Twenty? A dozen? How many rooms, how many square feet? How could Granny have kept track? A person could get lost.

And how did it happen that, after Grandfather died, it was Granny all by herself in a ratty hotel before she rented her flat, a one-bedroom "efficiency," where, with Mom once, in my twenties, I visited her? What had happened to the bank accounts? She shopped in the village, carried her groceries up the stairs. Talked about "going aloft."

Easy for my uncle to find her that December morning she didn't answer the phone. No halls to wander through. She left the flat immaculate, clean towels folded, the kitchen trash emptied. Tidy to the end. Told everyone her heart would stop on the 16th, and so it did. She'd destroyed her account books, all her calendars. Left no tracks, no record. Only a bag of bread crumbs by the sink, labeled "For the Birds."

∞

PERHAPS THE MAN

*in the boat is
only looking
down, struggling
to pull his oar
through dark water,
arm over arm,
one lift, one dip,
no time to glance
at the distant
hills, wonder where
this stream began.*

"ELEGANT," SHE SAID

My new friend was chuckling, saying she cracked up when I let fly
the "f" word while speaking to an audience

of five-hundred because, she said, I look so "elegant, a class act,
a knockout." I changed the subject. She doesn't

get it. In our family I'd always been the clumsy one, by sixth grade
inhabiting a close-to-six-foot, rib-protruding,

hunched-over frame, buck teeth in braces, wispy blonde hair, pale
bluish eyes. Called "Scarecrow," "String Bean,"

then in high school, "Boobless Bean." And with a regal-shouldered,
chocolate-eyed, russet-haired mother who

modeled for the fashion pages of *The Tucson Daily Citizen*. My little
sister, a brunette, "the pretty one," began

Flair Modeling School at fourteen. Those 1950s Clairol ads asked,
"Is it true blondes have more fun?" Not

this blonde. The time I brought my drawing of a girl to show
Daddy and his only comment was a clipped,

"She's not very pretty." Over my parents' Old Fashioneds, banter
about women: "pert little nose, a shame

about her piano legs"; "good-hearted, but that horrendous pitted
skin." Now the flesh of my arms droops like

crumpled silk. Yet my husband swears he loves my bones. Once,
when Mom was around my age, she spoke of

her granny Lilian Walker Graves, who sparkled on the vaudeville
stage. Men tripped on their shoe strings at

the sight of her, Mom said. "And my own mother," she went on,
"had that same quality, just as I did, and—as your

little sister does," she added, looking at the ceiling. But then, the year before Mom died in the retirement

    home, as I walked beside her electric cart while she steered past wheelchairs and walkers, a resident stopped us:

    "Why Pam," she gushed, "This daughter of yours—no one would question you're her mother! She looks just like you,

    moves with your elegance, your grace." Mom jerked upright and sputtered, "She *does*?" and pressed her foot on

    the accelerator, whizzing off. I had to run to catch up with her.

MAYBE HIS BOAT

*is drifting back
toward the mouth
of the river,
or he's grown tired
from the long push
and the banks down
farther lure him
with the fine silt
of easy slopes,
silky tendrils,
perhaps under
the mountains' mist
something hides he
fears he will reach.*

∞

MINING SILVER

Two hundred feet down, Catholic altars, shrines. Drilling into the rock, hard hats, face guards. Sometimes the molten magma is so rich in silver, the silver forces through the quartz crystal as silver wires. Looks almost like bent earrings, cheap, tired jewelry in the trash.

STIFF UPPER LIP

1.

Headlines in *The Evening Standard, Daily Telegraph, The Observer, The Daily Mirror, Sunday News, Daily Mail,* even *The Times*: "FIRE DESTROYS BATTLE ABBEY, 120 GIRLS AWAKENED BY ROAR OF FLAMES." And following: "Mrs. Jacoby, the headmistress, tells how, with splendid discipline, they tested new fire drill." Some young as eight, the oldest seventeen. January 1931. Mom would have been thirteen. The girls had practiced over and over. One girl would be tapped to wake the others, they'd all walk single-file downstairs and out the great front doors. "Clad in their nightclothes." Four in the morning. "Not one of them became hysterical." "The flames leapt to a height of a hundred feet." The fire burned on into the next day and the Abbot's Hall was reduced to a ruin. Built in 1066, Battle of Hastings. At six a.m., Mrs. Jacoby sent a telegraph to the parents of every girl: "All well."

2.

One hundred twenty girls in flannel dressing gowns crowding the courtyard, a January pre-dawn. One hundred nineteen girls' mummies and daddies coming for them the next day. Or the next—it would never do to leave Gladys (or Cynthia or Gwendolyn, or Edith, or Violet) in the midst of those horrid cinders, of course we'll bring the car, the poor dear, she must be dreadfully frightened.

But no one came for my mother. Because Granny was in Paris visiting a friend? Because Grandfather believed the telegram from Mrs. Jacoby saying "all" was "well"? No cell phones, no texting, no email, no way even to phone her daddy, ask him to please come, please. The tower fallen. All the mistresses returned home, even the one who taught French crossed the Channel back to Amiens. Alone with the housekeeper, the cook, and the gardener—the only girl left.

3.

How do you get back to the place above the staircase where the floor boards held? Where the wallpaper swirled with primroses, delphiniums, and petunias like the petals in your mummy's garden?

It was Wendy Flith, ten years old, who woke at four thirty, hot and thirsty, slipped to the bathroom for a drink of water, and smelled smoke. Thoroughly drilled, she blew her whistle, led the girls in her dorm room down the tower stairs. Meanwhile, Mrs. Hyndman had waked from the smoke, roused the rest. Timbers like bones, ribs protruding, the entire hall blazing.

4.

My mother rarely spoke of it. When she did, her accounts didn't vary, mirrored the newspapers'. Always, it was the girls' discipline she stressed, how they faced forward, eyes on the girl leading them down the stairs.

No mention of huddling with her favorite friends, no details of the nightclothes she was wearing (a red plaid robe? one with blue piping?), or the blouses, gone to cinders, she'd never wear again. Or how cold it was, so suddenly awake in the courtyard, waiting for the firemen. Watching flames pierce the Abbey's roof. Did she see the staircase crash to the stone floor as the last girl approached the open door? The papers' details were enough.

5.

Twenty years after Battle Abbey burned, the chair. Smoke in the night, my mother and father lifting the square wooden legs, tilting its bulk through the kitchen door. A cigarette dropped during the day, an ember bubbling through cloth and horse hair down to the metal springs. Out into the night. Her nylon nightgown, his seersucker pajamas, bare feet.

The smell stayed for days. They carried the chair back into the house, set it down in the living room, its blackened stuffing surrounding a ragged hole to stare down into—the padded arm a tangled chasm, its wiry innards coiled.

INTERIOR

Those Phoenix dust storms in the forties: a solid wall, brown mass hurtling toward us, as Mom screamed, "Close the windows, close the windows!" and we raced around the house, turning handles. Even so, after, a layer of dirt blurred the lines of every shelf and counter, every table, every cushion. Every book. The bathroom basin.

Where Granny on her visit helped me brush my teeth. Brisk little strokes around and around, up to the attic, she trilled, then to the nursery, down more stairs to the parlor, the drawing room, and, finally, all the way to the cellar. Rooms I'd never known existed.

What dust can do to the lungs—those fragile, spongy organs filled with alveoli. A struggle to breathe. These tiny spaces, miniature rooms within the duplex of the lungs.

Four rooms: two bedrooms, a kitchen, living room in that house. Smoke thickening the air. My father's five packs a day, my mother's half-dozen cigarettes with drinks before their dinner, when they talked and we were not to. In our cots in our room, strict seven o'clock bedtime for my sisters and me, no talking, no questions.

After Granny's visit, my own little mouth held polished hallways leading to rooms with windows glistening to moist lawns, a robin's-egg-blue sky. No dust. Or smoke. No need to open the rattling, rusted screen door to leave a choking house.

SILVER HANDLES, SPOUTS

Silversmiths form the pot first, then the handle. And of course, a pot needs a spout. Before the Ming Dynasty, people drank tea from clay bowls. The earliest teapots held only one serving, came from the Yixing region of China, fourteenth century, and you drank your tea directly from the spout.

Nobody ever says "born with a silver handle in her hand," though there's much fuss made about babies who slip into the world gumming silver spoons. Get a handle on it, we nag, handle it, get a grip. But no one mentions the necessity for handles on silver teapots. Without one, you'd burn your fingers pouring Earl Grey.

So much you shouldn't spout. The evening's dishes crashed on the kitchen floor, my mother's screaming, my father's raging, and the next day, not a word. The night my mother stood at the front door with a suitcase, nine-year-old me pulling at her skirt, sobbing, "Don't leave, Mommy, don't leave!" The next morning, over oatmeal, not a word.

It's complicated fitting a handle—or a spout—to a silver pot with bent shears, soldering and filing. How to move steaming liquids from interior spaces without harm? A slender trickle is always preferable to a torrid gush, especially if one is chatting in polite company. And how would you hold a scalding, heavy pot in your hand without a sturdy handle and a clear spout, a way to lighten the weight inside?

LATENT IMAGE

Before she died, Mom pulled that photo out of the album, tore it to shreds. The one that showed her at seven, naked, posed like a nymph, a statue on the lawn. Grandfather's insisting she strip in front of the servants and sit like that, her legs folded to one side, her head bent in the opposite direction. His little nymph.

Stilled, in that photo, caught by silver particles, the standard black and white photographic process introduced in 1871. A photo's final image: metallic silver embedded in a gelatin coating.

"Stills," we say, stopped action, a single frame of a film. Yet I never knew Mom stilled until she died, her trim body beneath a sheet. Always moving, vacuuming every crumb of dust to be sucked into the guts of the Electrolux, its bag emptied into the garbage and gone. After dinner, Ed Sullivan on TV, her hands working a needle or scissors, her feet joggling, toes wriggling. Daytime, her sewing machine's roar, her fingers zipping the fabric toward the needle, her foot pressing the pedal, full speed. And driving, always over the limit, as if to say "get me out of here."

Silver atoms, freed when silver salts meet the light, form an image that's stable. Once the film's developed, it's bathed in a chemical fixer. Clean water clears the fixer from the print, and the latent image becomes permanent.

The story she told me long after I'd moved away: how, when, at thirteen, she asked her mother what she should do about the black hairs spiralling in her armpits, Granny said, "Father can help you with that," and he did, in the shower, every week, shaving her.

∞

BUT EVEN THESE

*stones at the base
of the scroll may
be less rounded,
sharper than they
appear, jagged
edges may loom
underwater,
threatening this
too narrow boat.*

SURGERY, A LITTLE HISTORY

Stunned by the god's "feathered glory," Yeats wrote
    of Leda, in one of my mother's favorite poems. How many
        painters have rendered this image, of a woman swooning
with a swan. But the trickery, the deceit of Zeus,
    disguising himself. And now, these doctors of mine,
        with their downy reassurance. Robotic surgery, they coo,
easy as slipping into and out of a pond. Not gods,
    but white-coated, so feathery-voiced I believe them,
        sign the forms. Their sleek offices, paintings of lakes,
of cool streams on their walls. Such calming
    waters I lie back, feet propped in the metal stirrups,
        till the speculum is pressed inside, probing for what lies
underneath: stems of water lilies, small
    fish. Scraping the silt. No "sudden blow," the surgeons
        promise, "minimally invasive, laparoscopic, tiny incisions,
needle-thin instruments. Nothing to fear,"
    they stress. But photos I've now seen online show
        massive silvery cones, spiked bills that angle like spears
toward the bull's eye of a belly. "Indifferent"
    beaks that peck around inside, pulling sagging
        organs upright, shoving them into new places, wrapping
them in mesh like the webs between toes of
    swans. "A month," they say. But it's more like
        twenty before my body's mine again, works again, though
I'm told I'm a lucky one, patients half
    my age may need a catheter for a year, even two,
        "post-op," and often, they add, women will need

the surgery redone. We say we're "put under"
    an anesthetic. And now that Mom's been gone
        ten years, I'm sinking down into murk to remember
the time during eighth grade when she
    picked me up, surprising me after school, my gray
        Samsonite packed in the Ford's back seat: "We're going
to the hospital, honey, just a little operation,
    so you won't have those awful cramps anymore." After
        the nurse stripped me and tied me into a blue robe that left
my bottom bare, she told my mother
    to leave. They swooped in then, medical students,
        checking for cancer, they said, and pulled aside the gown,
fingered my breasts. The next morning,
    the nurse wheeled me down the hall for the little
        operation. The doctor and his white-jacketed flock were
waiting, thought the anesthetic had
    kicked in. I was awake all during their hooting,
        their laughing. Spread-eagled in the stirrups, the clamp
inside, the scraping. No Yeatsian
    "white rush." The blood that followed. Mom
        never knew. Shortly before she died, she told me how,
the first year she was married, her doctor
    insisted she come to the office Saturday morning. Got
        her on her back, fiddled with her clitoris, diddled her, his
fingers pulsing inside her, experimenting, to
    make her come. The same ob/gyn who delivered me,
        who believed women should suffer in childbirth, no need

for an anesthetic while he rammed those forceps
    deep inside to haul me out. The body holds these
        incisions. For years. And genetic memory exists: we carry
molecular scars. No eggs from such visitations. Only
    hard-boiled knowledge that you won't get the truth
        from these hook-scissored beaks when what they do is tear,
rip into you, and maybe, maybe you'll recover,
    put on new knowledge with your own power. Flap
        back at them, beat your own wings against them. And snap.

HOW A SURFACE

can gleam in light,
a crystalline
slice, so you think
you can avoid
going under.

∞

THE SILVER TUREEN (3)

Company coming, close it, push it to the back of the counter. All those papery shreds of garlic skins I should have cleaned out. Maybe place the old crystal vase filled with roses in front, so no one will even notice the tureen, ask about it.

All the photos, everyone lined up, arms around arms, mouths stretched in endless smiles. The albums we keep, the posing.

NOW I LEARN

The story about Great Grandfather sailing up the Yangtze: false. I've found a volume from Oxford University Press, as well as files in the London Metropolitan Archives setting the record straight. And in a cardboard box buried in a closet: a blue cloth-bound book my grandfather published in 1958, *The House of Dodwell*. It's even on Wikipedia.

William R. Adamson was the man who, in 1852, came back from China with a ship loaded with silk and the embryo of a fortune. George Benjamin Dodwell would have been only a year old. Later, at twenty, he signed on as a clerk in the Shanghai office. By 1899 he'd been elected Chairman of the Board, the company renamed for him.

How did I get this wrong? Had I embellished, exaggerated the tale? Had Mom? Because it had a more silvery sheen?

GATHERING BONES

Like a book, Mom said about life: you turn the page and go on. The same way she moved in and out of houses. Garage sale after sale. Each year like a chapter torn from a novel's spine and hurled.

But some of us go back, looking for patterns. The way a plot builds, chapter upon chapter, like a pelvis resting on the femur, femur on the patella, on the tibia and fibula.

That film I can't forget: *Aftermath*, story of a Catholic Polish farmer who discovers Jewish tombstones buried under the town's road. He's obsessed with digging them up, five-foot, rounded headstones, one by one. Doesn't know why. He plants them in rows, like corn, in his field. Learns Hebrew, reads the inscriptions, names and names.

During the months before she died, when I begged her to talk about her childhood, my mother changed the subject, demanded more milk in her tea.

Let sleeping dogs lie, the villagers, even the young priest, warned that farmer.

Years ago, Mom told me about a nightmare. She was racing, breathless, through a walled, labyrinthian garden to save herself from a gigantic man. How many houses had it taken to escape? New Jersey, Arizona, house after house, different towns, and finally, in less than a decade, three houses in New Hampshire. Each one repainted.

At the film's end, the farmer learns it was his father who'd led the villagers in a round-up of the local Jews, locking them in the family's cottage, which he set on fire.

The night before the family's ceremonial scattering of Mom's ashes on the lake she'd loved, I slept with the cannister beside me. Sunrise, I carried it down to the dock, opened the lid. I reached in, gathered a small handful, and over my arms and legs spread powdery flakes of crushed bone. I slipped then, into the water that carried them, glittering, in the light.

Once I'd dreamed of myself as a toddler, walking down an unlit hospital hall with closed doors on both sides. I was holding my mother's hand. But no, she was gripping mine.

FOLDINGS

Packing for his return to England, Grandfather showed me how to roll socks into little fists, tuck them into shoes, fold shirts into rectangles tidy as sealed envelopes. I was three. His suitcase a marvel of geometric shapes. Key twisted in the suitcase lock.

I'm folding sheets now, smoothing squares into smaller squares so they'll nestle at right angles on the linen closet shelf. I was six when Granny showed me how to iron without an iron, "finger pressing," she called it. How to smooth the wrinkled, still-damp fabric of a skirt or blouse with the flat of your hands.

That July when Mom called, took a half hour to tell me what she'd stuffed so deep in a trunk it had taken decades to uncover. She said she'd finally remembered: nighttimes, in the big bed, her little-girl self folded between them, her daddy played with her, taught her to play with him, her mummy, wide awake, right there.

How you can fold yourself in on yourself. The toes of the socks curl innermost, the tops wrapping around them. How you can take your own layers and tuck them into creases.

Grandfather's origami—on his second visit, he showed us how to press plain white paper into tiny triangles, and then—voilà!—open a flower, a bird.

A different kind of folding. And unfolding. The way you shake a clean sheet till it sails over the bed, billows. The way a white-winged dove folds her wings close to her rounded middle, then opens them out, lifts off. Unfoldings, the way a flock of swallows makes pin pricks in the sky, openings.

Last summer in Paris, at the Centre Pompidou—the paintings of Simon Hantaï, wide white walls with his room-sized unfoldings. He'd crushed the canvases, folded the cloth so he couldn't see the whole surface while he brushed the paint. Pliage. Said he didn't want to know where the edge was, where the canvas stopped.

HER LISTS

Four times in my life I saw her. And can't forget the way, afternoons, Granny sat upright on the sofa doing her "accounts." Checking items off lists. Long lists, though she was a guest, not even housework to supervise, no shopping needed, no doctors' appointments while away from England.

Both my sisters and I make lists—we'll even add an item once a chore is completed, simply for the pleasure of crossing it off. Little checks, like sketches of birds in flight.

For years Granny would have had much to keep track of—the sprawling hilltop mansion in Hong Kong, another house in Shanghai, a country manor near Windsor, a London townhouse. Scores of servants to oversee. Laundry lists. With every move, the ivory, the china, and the silver all properly packed, accounted for in the next new place. Lists upon lists.

And a list of lessons for her daughter: The best way to thread a needle, how to mend a rip in a silk skirt. How to wear a veiled hat, arrange the feather so it cocked enticingly.

Were there lists under the lists? Items like: "Write Cousin Stanley in Hong Kong, inquire whether we could send dear Pamela for a year or two."

Was it she who encouraged her own child to do with Grandfather what she couldn't bring herself to, so he'd leave her, his wife, alone? Or did she think a little girl should be trained in the arts of the bed, be prepared for what would follow? Or—was it that, as his wife, she knew her duty: to satisfy a husband's desires.

And which one of them insisted Mom leave for Hong Kong when she turned seventeen?

When Granny used to faint during fancy dinners, Mom told me, guests thought she was just being dramatic. Yet when the list you can't write down constricts your spine, how do you stay upright? Check marks like wings. But no feathers could carry such weight.

INCEST

This story has a hundred beginnings. The best old British tradition. No horses were frightened. There were no horses.

BIRD SONGS

Turned into birds, those sisters: Procne, Philomela, a nightingale and a swallow. Oh swallow swallow, hovering as the dark drops, nesting in the rafters, hidden places. How Philomela's threads told the story. Without a tongue.

My mother's sewing, her foot clamped on that pedal, racing the Singer's steel needle through the cloth. The skirts she made, heavy with braid, rows and rows of rick-rack, silver, copper, black. And her jewelry that clanked, metallic, like armor.

These stories no one speaks. How we're silenced, mute. Procne unaware her husband raped her sister, till Philomela's weaving told the tale.

Mom's skirts, voluminous. Yards and yards of her own seaming. And necklaces that roped around her throat and chest, jangling. While lying in the sun, slathered with lotion. All covered up one way or another. High-necked blouses, stiletto heels that clanked on the concrete floor.

Even smothered, a story won't die. Centuries, characters shift, but not the plot. How you know and you don't know. Enough for now to say: my sisters and I—grown daughters of that mother, all skilled with colored threads, with embroidering our own patterns on cloth, and each of us harboring birds. No nightingales in our country, but oh, the swallows, nesting, safe among the wooden bones, timbers of an old, old house.

∞

PERHAPS UPSTREAM

*the water grows
calmer, cleaner,
perhaps there you'll
see down into
the riverbed,
where small fish might
flicker among
crevices, moss
wisping among
cold granite stones.*

BEYOND A CERTAIN AGE, I LOOK FOR PARIS IN PARIS

I know about le Syndrome de Paris, triggered when a greenhorn's
    rosy-lensed image turns muddy, but I'm no wistful
        Francophile neophyte, so why am I
feeling like my British uncle who'd sniped as I left for my first trip
    to Paris: "Why bother with that filth?" When
        my friends heard I was heading
again for the City of Lights, they said "Paris? *oh! yes!*" in a breathy,
    pre-orgasmic voice, as if they were picturing my
        lounging outside a café on
the Boul'Mich over a café au lait or glass of chilled Sauvignon Blanc
    as prelude to a blissful night with my husband in
        a cramped but oh, so charming
chambre double, forgetting that I can't do caffeine or alcohol, and
    that, as I'd also forgotten, in mid-July the sidewalks,
        the Métro, and the galleries would
be chock-a-block with chattering Brits, Italians, Yanks, Germans,
    and Brazilians, along with—since it's the week
        of the Tour de France—clusters
of steel-bodied cyclists, so we're jostled by tee-shirts emblazoned
    with slogans like "Endurance Conspiracy" and
        "Tourminator." The outing we'd
planned to Giverny is canceled, too much traffic, when for months
    I've been yearning to peer down into the waters that
        spawned Monet's *Nymphéas:*
those rounded walls in l'Orangerie, depths that lead to more depths,
    dissolving boundaries. Where is the Paris of my mother's
        rebellious cousin who painted with

Max Ernst, or the Paris of my grad student and her new husband,
    noses nuzzling before la tour Eiffel on their
        Facebook post? Or the Paris
of my twenties, when I first floated into Monet's water lilies, when
    the Seine glimmered like a thousand liquid candles
        as I sauntered across Pont Marie
at midnight. On l'Avenue de Clichy, on Rue de Rivoli, I see only
    dog poop, crumpled plastic bags, and unfiltered
        butts. A two-hour wait to enter
Notre Dame, the façade blocked by tawdry bleachers. Pebbles
    from the Tuileries have collected in my sandals
        though I keep jiggling my feet
to shake them out. Maybe I have actually become my British
    uncle. Samuel Johnson said if you're tired
        of London, you're tired
of life. I'll bet he'd put Paris in the same category—after all, didn't
    he say French faces shine with "a thousand
        Graces"? I can't begin to
keep up with my mountain-goat, marathoner husband who'll
    cover seven arrondissements on foot at
        a greyhound's trot. Yet
now, on the day before leaving, I'm fueled by a breakfast of hard
    boiled eggs, and he says, how about Sacré Coeur,
        it's only a ten-minute walk,
we'll take our time. So we do, and the hill with its rounded, gleaming
    white cathedral is washed with breezes. Inside
        les Jardins Renoir, we are

alone in the courtyard, red poppies brimming at green edges of
>   stones, a silence glistening through sudden empty
>   space. And here it is: not Giverny,
but a round pond, and, *oh! yes!* pink and white water lilies, their
>   shimmering pads like clean hands open to sky,
>   stems trailing into the barely
visible muck, and tiny speckled fish burbling to the surface, then
>   spiraling back down to the silt, murky depths,
>   the dirt that underlies us all.

THE SCROLL'S LANDSCAPE

is black and white,
the foreground trees'
thin strokes like scars
creasing the shore,
while only from
a distance will
the high mountains,
adrift in mist,
appear silver.

ACKNOWLEDGMENTS

I am grateful to the editors of the following magazines, in which some of these poems first appeared, at times in slightly different versions.

Diode   "Silver Handles, Spouts"

Exit 7   "On the Chinese Scroll,"
"Or Did I Mistake," "Is His Boat Strong,"
"Perhaps the Man," and "I Hadn't Seen"

Ilanot Review   "Ivory Carvings"

Matter Press   "Below the Salt,"
"Treading the Boards," and "Stiff Upper Lip"

Nimrod International Journal   "Foldings," "The Scroll's Landscape,"
and "This Far Downstream"

Prairie Schooner   "Surgery, a Little History,"

Plume   "On the RMS Queen Mary,"
"Latent Image," "'Elegant,' She Said,"
"Sunday Lunch at Mom's Cousin Dinnie's: June, 1969,"
"Her Lists," "Little Pieces of String," "Bird Songs," and "Incest"

Poetry Bay   "Along a River," "How A Surface,"
"Perhaps Upstream," and "Maybe His Boat"

Seneca Review   Published as sections of a lyric essay,
"Silver Sequence": "Silver Mining,"
"The Silver Tureen (1)," "The Silver Tureen (2),"
and "The Silver Tureen (3)"

The Southern Review   "Interior," "Silk Roads,"
and "What Surfaces"

Superstition Review   "Gathering Bones"

Valparaiso Poetry Review   "Beyond a Certain Age, I Look for Paris in Paris"

"Gathering Bones" was reprinted in *Women's Voices for Change,* Poetry Editor, Rebecca Foust, (http://womensvoicesforchange.org/tag/poetry-sunday, 2015).

"'Elegant,' She Said" was reprinted in *Nasty Women Poets*, Editors, Grace Bauer and Julie Kane, Lost Horse Press, 2017.

"On the Chinese Scroll," "Along a River," "This Far Downstream," "Is His Boat Strong," "Perhaps the Man," "Maybe His Boat," "But Even These," "How a Surface," "Perhaps Upstream," and "The Scroll's Landscape" are included in *Shimmer*, a chapbook, Glass Lyre Press, 2019.

So many friends helped with this manuscript in its many stages, especially Kevin Clark and Hannah Stein, as well as Ralph Black, Michele Flom, Alice Friman, Sarah Grieve, Barbara Hamby, and Jacqueline Kolosov. I'm also grateful to Natasha Lvovitch, David Dooley, and Kacee Belcher for help with some of the individual poems included in the book, and I want to thank Joel Peckham and Terry Lucas for extremely helpful advice. I am everlastingly thankful for my two amazing sisters, Patricia McConnell and Liza Piatt, whose stories and encouragement helped birth this book. I am also supremely grateful for the understanding and support of my wonderful son and daughter-in-law David and Kayo Barker. And how ever to thank my patient, brilliant husband, Steven G. Kellman, who read and reread—and reread—draft upon draft of these poems?

Wendy Barker's sixth collection of poetry, *One Blackbird at a Time,* received the John Ciardi Prize for Poetry (BkMk Press, 2015). Her fifth chapbook is *Shimmer* (Glass Lyre Press, 2019). An anthology of poems about the 1960s, *Far Out: Poems of the '60s*, co-edited with Dave Parsons, was released by Wings Press in 2016. Other books include a selection of poems with accompanying essays, *Poems' Progress* (Absey & Co., 2002), and a selection of translations, *Rabindranath Tagore: Final Poems* (co-translated with Saranindranath Tagore, Braziller, 2001). Her poems have appeared in numerous journals and anthologies including *The Southern Review, Nimrod, New Letters, Poetry, Prairie Schooner,* and *Plume,* as well as *The Best American Poetry 2013*. She is the author of *Lunacy of Light: Emily Dickinson and the Experience of Metaphor* (Southern Illinois University Press, 1987), as well as co-editor (with Sandra M. Gilbert) of *The House is Made of Poetry: The Art of Ruth Stone* (Southern Illinois University Press, 1996). Recipient of NEA and Rockefeller fellowships among other awards, she is the Pearl LeWinn Endowed Chair and Poet-in-Residence at the University of Texas at San Antonio, where she has taught since 1982. Wendy is married to the critic, biographer, essayist, and poet Steven G. Kellman.

Typefaces Used:

TYPEFACE GARAMOND – Garamond
TYPEFACE: PERPETUA TITLING MT – LIGHT

CPSIA information can be obtained
at www.ICGtesting.com
Printed in the USA
FSHW021351140120
66050FS